Friends

May You Always Have Loving Friendships

⌧ HAZELDEN®
Keep Coming Back™

Created by Meiji Stewart
Illustrated by David Blaisdell

Friends
© 2000 by Meiji Stewart

ISBN# 1-56838-515-3

Hazelden
P.O. Box 176
15251 Pleasant Valley Road
Center City, MN 55012-0176
1-800-328-9000
www.hazelden.org

Illustration: David Blaisdell, Tucson, Arizona
Cover design: Kahn Design, Encinitas, California

Dedicated to old friends and new ones to come:
Stuart, Colin, Bruce, David, Nori, Hayley, Tim, Robbi, Robin, Carol,
Mustafa, Hassan, Levent, Jay, Maria, Brittany, Jeff, Annabelle, Elena,
Grant, Jacqui, Simon, Ray, Leslie, Sam, Anne, Jim, Tammy, John, Christian,
Astrid, Nancy, Susan, Art, Happy Bear, Jeff, Pete, Sarah, Gary, Marianne,
and of course my best friend and soul mate, Claudia.

Thanks to:
David for the wonderful illustrations. I was blessed to be able to work with
him. Thanks also to Roger and Darryl for putting it all together, almost
always under deadline (usually yesterday). Thanks to Jeff for the beautiful
book cover. Thanks to Gay, Jane, Regina, Zane, and especially Neill for
making it possible to bring these books to press. Special thanks to my
daughter, Malia, and stepson, Tommy, for teaching me how to love and
laugh lots and not take life too seriously...as do Star, Oliver, and Jewel.

If I had a single flower for every time
I think about you, I could walk forever
in my garden.

Claudia Grandi

How do you do—
would you like to be friends?

Janis Ian

4

A friend will joyfully sing with you when you are on the mountaintop and silently walk beside you through the valley.

As a kid I learned that my brother and I could walk forever on a railroad track and never fall off—if we just reached across the track and held each other's hand.

Steve Potter

Love cannot be wasted. It makes no difference where it is bestowed; it always brings in big returns.

If you don't look out for others, who will look out for you?
Whoopi Goldberg

If you have a friend worth loving,
love them.

Never part without loving words to think of
during your absence. It may be that you will
not meet again in life.

Jean Paul

If we all discovered that we had only five minutes left to say all that we wanted to say, every telephone booth would be occupied by people calling other people to tell them that they loved them. *Christopher Morley*

Fortify yourself with a flock of friends! You can select them at random, write to one, dine with one, visit one, or take your problems to one. There is always at least one who will understand, inspire, and give you the lift you may need at the time.

George Matthew Adams

Shared joy is double joy; shared sorrow is half sorrow.
Swedish Proverb

I don't sing because I'm happy.
I'm happy because I sing.

The words of the tongue should have three
gatekeepers: Is it true? Is it kind?
Is it necessary?

Arab Proverb

"Stay" is a charming word in a friend's vocabulary.
Louisa May Alcott

Good friends are good for your health.

Irwin Sarason

What sunshine is to flowers, smiles are to
humanity. They are but trifles, to be sure,
but, scattered along life's pathway,
the good they do is inconceivable.

Joseph Addison

14

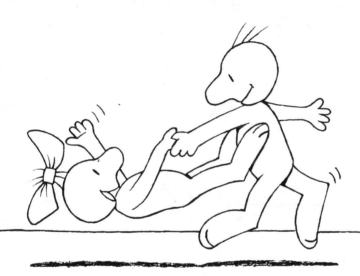

"On with the dance, let joy be unconfined" is my motto,
whether there's any dance to dance or any joy to unconfine.
Mark Twain

We should seize every opportunity to give encouragement. Encouragement is oxygen to the soul.

George Matthew Adams

Love lights more fires than hate extinguishes.

Ella Wheeler Wilcox

Was she so loved because her eyes were so beautiful or were her eyes so beautiful because she was so loved.

Anzia Yezierska

The best thing to hold on to in this world is each other.

Linda Ellerbee

Love Is...

the *A*nswer, whatever the question.

*B*eing there to wipe away the tears.

a *C*hoice, color the world beautiful.

*D*oing, actions speak louder than words.

*E*verywhere, if you look for it.

*F*orgiving and for giving.

*G*ratitude, for all that is, was, and will be.

*H*olding hands more, hurrying less.

*I*nclusive, not exclusive.

*J*ourneying together on our own paths.

*K*indness, do what you can when you can.

*L*aughing, listening, and letting go.

*M*agical, the more you give, the more you receive.

*N*ow, why wait until tomorrow?

*O*pen-minded, there are many sides to every story.

*P*owerful, be the cause of wonderful things.

*Q*uick to build bridges and take down walls.

*R*ealizing you wouldn't want it any other way.

*S*haring, dare to care.

*T*houghtful, tender, and true.

*U*nconditional, no ifs, ands or buts.

*V*ital, like sunshine and rain to a flower.

*W*illingness to see through the eyes of a child.

*X*pressing your truth, knowing the answers will come.

*Y*earning for connection, not correction.

*Z*any, dive deep into the mystery.

©Meiji Stewart

18

There is only one happiness in life,
to love and be loved. *George Sand*

Love is the stuff that life is made of.

The one thing we can never get
enough of is love. And the one thing
we never give enough is love.

Henry Miller

When you were born, God said, "Yes!"

I expect to pass through life but once. If therefore, there can be any kindness I can show, or any good thing I can do to any fellow human being, let me do it now, and not defer or neglect it, as I shall not pass this way again.

William Penn

Some people come into our lives and quietly go; others stay for a while and leave footprints on our hearts and we are never the same.

No road is long with good company. *Turkish Proverb*

Friendship is the inexpressible comfort of feeling safe with a person, having neither to weigh thoughts nor measure words.

George Eliot

The door to your heart can be opened only from the inside.

The sight of you is good for sore eyes. *Jonathan Swift*

So long as we love we serve; so long as we are
loved by others, I would almost say we are
indispensable; and no man
is useless while he has a friend.

Robert Louis Stevenson

Don't walk in front of me, I may not always follow.
Don't walk behind me, I may not always lead.
Just walk beside me and be my friend.

Savor life's tiny delights—a crackling fire, a glorious sunset,
a hug from a child, a walk with a friend, a kiss behind
the ear. *John Anthony*

Friendship is not a sometime thing.

Outside of a dog, a book is man's best friend.
Inside of a dog, it's too dark to read.

Groucho Marx

When you dig another out of their troubles,
you find a place to bury your own.

May the sun always shine on your windowpane;
May a rainbow be certain to follow each rain.
May the hand of a friend always be near you;
May God fill your heart with gladness to cheer you.

Irish Blessing

Everybody needs a friend.

If you begin to live life looking for all the good
that is around you, you will find joy
everywhere.

Let us be first to give a friendly sign,
to nod first, smile first, speak first,
and if such a thing is necessary—
forgive first.

Fear makes strangers of people
who should be friends.

Shirley MacLaine

Good friends always make us feel like winners,
even when we've just lost. *William Arthur Ward*

It is better to be happy than to be right.

No matter where we are, we need those
friends who trudge across from
their neighborhoods to ours.

Stephen Peters

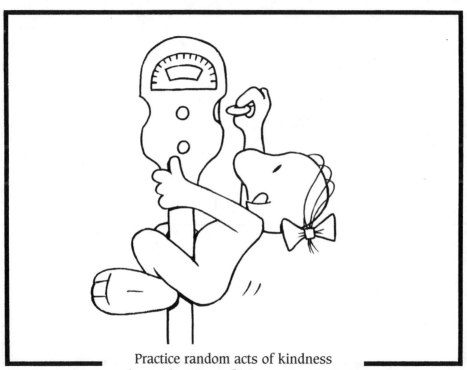

Practice random acts of kindness
and senseless acts of beauty. *Ann Herbert*

There is no desire so deep as the simple desire
for companionship.

Graham Greene

The most I can do for my friend is simply
to be his friend.

Henry David Thoreau

It is not so much our friends' help that helps us as the confident knowledge that they will help us. *Epicurus*

To have a good friend is one of the highest delights of life; to be a good friend is one of the noblest and most difficult undertakings.

My friends are an oasis to me, encouraging me to go on. They are essential to my well-being.

Dee Brestin

A friend is someone who knows your song and sings it to you when you forget. *Eric Spiess*

I thank God, my friend, for the blessing you are...for the joy of your laughter...the comfort of your prayers...the warmth of your smile.

Treasure the love you receive above all.
It will survive long after your gold and
good health have vanished.

Og Mandino

There is no physician like a true friend.

One of the things I keep learning is that the secret of being happy is doing things for other people.

Dick Gregory

Your task is not to seek for love, but to find the barriers in yourself that you have built against it.

A Course in Miracles

Help your brother's boat across, and your own will reach the shore. *Hindi Proverb*

I still find each day too short for all the
thoughts I want to think, all the walks I want
to take, all the books I want to read, and all
the friends I want to see. The longer I live, the
more my mind dwells upon the beauty and the
wonder of the world.

John Burroughs

The World is a great mirror.
It reflects back to you what you are.
If you are loving, if you are friendly,
if you are helpful,
the World will prove loving and
friendly and helpful to you.
The World is what you are.

Thomas Dreier

You Are...

*A*mazing, the architect of your destiny.

*B*eautiful, both inside and out.

*C*ourageous, being true to yourself.

*D*ynamic, ever changing and growing.

*E*nthusiastic about living and loving life.

*F*allible, perfectly imperfect.

*G*rateful for each and every day.

*H*ealthy, full of energy.

*I*ntuitive, looking within for guidance.

*J*oyful, happy to be you.

*K*indhearted, reaching out to others.

*L*ovable, exactly as you are.

*M*iraculous, a child of the universe.

*N*ow here, fully in this moment.

*O*ptimistic, anything is possible.

*P*owerful, beyond imagination.

*Q*uick to build bridges not walls.

*R*esourceful, obstacles are stepping stones.

*S*piritual, having a human experience.

*T*rustworthy, speaking from your heart.

*U*nique and unrepeatable.

*V*aluable, you make a difference.

*W*ise, open to all of life's lessons.

*X*cited about pursuing your dreams.

*Y*oung at heart, delightfully childlike.

*Z*any, with a great sense of humor.

©*Meiji Stewart*

46

There is no need to go to India or anywhere else to find peace. You will find that deep place of silence right in your room, your garden or even your bathtub.
Elisabeth Kübler-Ross

One close friend is worth more than a
thousand acquaintances.

Friendship with oneself is all important,
because without it one cannot be friends with
anyone else in the world.

Eleanor Roosevelt

Friends are gifts, unwrap them. *Meiji Stewart*

If you were arrested
for being a loving friend, would there be
enough evidence to convict you?

Those who bring sunshine to the lives of others cannot keep it from themselves. *James M. Barrie*

A true friend unbosoms freely, advises justly,
assists readily, adventures boldly, takes all
patiently, defends courageously, and continues
a friend unchangeably.

William Penn

The most important medicine
is tender love and care.

Mother Teresa

I'm so glad you are here....It helps me to realize
how beautiful my world is. *Rainer Maria Rilke*

Each friend represents a world in us, a world possibly not born until they arrive, and it is only by this meeting that a new world is born.

Anaïs Nin

Meeting someone for the first time is like going on a treasure hunt. What wonderful worlds we can find in others!

Edward E. Ford

One of the advantages of being disorderly is that one is
constantly making exciting discoveries. *A. A. Milne*

It's your love your friends need—never expensive gifts or extravagant surprises.

Marion Garretty

A faithful friend is the medicine of life.

Ecclesiastes

Small tokens of love carry messages far beyond their size.
Karl-Hans von Fremde

Today say "I love you" to those you love.
The eternal silence is long enough to be silent
in, and that awaits us all.

George Eliot

Friendship is precious, not only in the shade,
but in the sunshine of life.

Thomas Jefferson

Never does a man describe
his own character more clearly
than by his way of describing
that of others.

Jean Paul

Friendliness is contagious.

Donald Laird

Life is fortified by many friendships.
To love, and to be loved, is the greatest
happiness of existence.

Sydney Smith

Sticks in a bundle are unbreakable.

Kenyan Proverb

Life is like the car pool lane. The only way to get to your destination quickly is to take some people with you. *Peter Ward*

I have learned that to have a good friend is the purest of all God's gifts, for it is love that has no exchange of payment.

Frances Farmer

We should behave to our friends as we would wish our friends to behave to us.

Aristotle

Do not use a hatchet to remove a fly from your friend's forehead. *Chinese Proverb*

The Eskimos had fifty-two names for
snow because snow was important to
them; there ought to be as many for love.

Margaret Atwood

Friends are the family you have chosen.

There are good ships and there are bad ships,
but the best ships are friendships. *Cicero*

It's the friends you can call up at 4 A.M. that matter.

Marlene Dietrich

Knowing what to say is not always necessary; just the presence of a caring friend can make a world of difference.

Sheri Curry

A true friend is a "fowl" weather friend. *Meiji Stewart*

You will find as you look back upon your life that the moments when you have really lived are the moments when you have done things in the spirit of love.

Henry Drummond

Nothing, so long as I am in my senses, would match with the joy that a friend may bring.

Horace

A good friend never gets in your way
unless you're on your way down.

I count your friendship one of the chiefest pleasures of my life, a comfort in time of doubt and trouble, a joy in time of prosperity and success, and an inspiration at all times.

Edwin Osgood Grover

There isn't much that I can do,
But I can share my flowers with you,
And I can share my books with you,
And sometimes share your burdens too...
As on our way we go.

Maude V. Preston

There is no joy in life like the joy of sharing. *Billy Graham*

One little act of kindness is better than
feelings of love for all mankind.

Marie Scaletty

Getting things accomplished isn't nearly
as important as taking time for love.

Janette Oke

What do we live for, if it is not to make life less difficult for each other?

George Eliot

If you approach each new person you meet in a spirit of adventure, you will find yourself endlessly fascinated by new channels of thought and experience and personality that you encounter.

Eleanor Roosevelt

Friends Are...

*A*mazing, cherish them.

*B*lessings, acknowledge them.

*C*aring, allow them.

*D*ependable, rely on them.

*E*ncouraging, hear them.

*F*allible, love them.

*G*ifts, unwrap them.

*H*ealing, be with them.

*I*mportant, value them.

*J*uicy, savor them.

*K*ind, delight in them.

*L*oyal, mirror them.

*M*agical, soar with them.

*N*ecessary, cultivate them.

*O*ptimistic, support them.

*P*riceless, treasure them.

*Q*uirky, enjoy them.

*R*are, hold on to them.

*S*trong, lean on them.

*T*eachers, learn from them.

*U*nderstanding, talk to them.

*V*ulnerable, embrace them.

*W*armhearted, listen to them.

*X*traordinary, recognize them.

*Y*oung at heart, play with them.

*Z*any, laugh with them.

©Meiji Stewart

Friendship is a sheltering tree. *Samuel Taylor Coleridge*

Friendship? Yes, please.

Charles Dickens

The greatest good you can do for another is not just to
share your riches, but to reveal to him his own.

Benjamin Disraeli

A cup of tea, a prayer or two, blessed
moments shared with you. *Ellen Cuomo*

Snowflakes are one of nature's most fragile things, but just look what they can do when they stick together.

Vesta M. Kelly

No love, no friendship can cross the path of our destiny without leaving some mark on it forever.

François Mauriac

Hold a true friend with both your hands. *Nigerian Proverb*

A friend is able to see you as the wonderful
person God created you to be.

Ann D. Parrish

Everyone needs someone
who he feels listens to him.

C. Neil Strait

80

The chief danger in life is that you may take too many precautions. *Alfred Adler*

We are each of us angels with only one wing,
and we can only fly embracing each other.

Luciano de Crescenzo

Tell me whom you frequent,
and I will tell you who you are.

French Proverb

Trouble is a sieve through which we sift our acquaintances.
Those too big to pass through are our friends. *Arlene Francis*

If I don't have friends, then I ain't got nothin'.

Billie Holiday

Everybody is somebody's friend.
How would you want your friends treated?

Friendship comes in all sizes, colors and ways. *Irma*

We should not look at or listen to the one we feel is making us angry and causing us to suffer. In fact, the main root of our suffering is the seed of anger in us. The other person may have said or done something unskillful or unmindful. But his unskillful words or actions arise from his own suffering. He may just be seeking some relief, hoping to survive. The excessive suffering of one person will very often overflow onto others. A person who is suffering needs our help, not our anger.

Thich Nhat Hanh

Am I united with my friend in heart?
What matters if our place be wide apart?

Anwar-I Suheili

My friend is not perfect
—no more than I am—
and so we suit each other admirably.

Alexander Smith

87

A true friend is someone who is there for you
when he'd rather be anywhere else.

Len Wein

Friendship is a plant which must
be often watered.

If a friend is in trouble, don't annoy him by asking
if there is anything you can do. Think up something
appropriate and do it. *Edgar W. Howe*

Be a friend, the rest will follow.

Emily Dickinson

Remember, we all stumble,
every one of us.
That's why it's a comfort to go
hand in hand.

Emily Kimbrough

It seems to me that trying to live without friends is like milking a bear to get cream for your morning coffee. It is a whole lot of trouble, and then not worth much after you get it.

Zora Neale Hurston

Love is, above all, the gift of oneself.

Jean Anouilh

What you give—you get.
What you send out—comes back.
What you sow—you reap.

Weigh the true advantages of forgiveness and resentment to the heart. Then choose. *Jack Kornfield*

Treat your friends as you do your pictures,
and place them in their best light.

Jennie Jerome Churchill

The greatest weakness of most humans is their
hesitancy to tell others how much they love
them while they're still alive.

O. A. Battista

If we give someone a piece of bread and butter,
that's kindness, but if we put jelly or peanut butter
on it, then it's loving kindness.

There is more hunger for love and
appreciation in this world than for bread.

Mother Teresa

Without true friends,
the world is but a wilderness.

Francis Bacon

Every morning is a fresh opportunity to find God's extraordinary joy in the most ordinary places. *Janet L. Weaver*

Blessed is the influence of one true,
loving, human soul on another.

George Eliot

No person is your friend who demands your
silence, or denies your right to grow.

Alice Walker

Hear me! A single twig breaks, but the
bundle of twigs is strong. *Tecumseh*

The less you open your heart to others,
the more your heart suffers.

Deepak Chopra

Love everybody you love; you can never tell
when they might not be there.

Nancy Bush Ellis

I like not only to be loved, but to be told that I am loved; the realm of silence is large enough beyond the grave.

George Eliot

Take time today to call or send a grateful message to a friend.

William Arthur Ward

Loving Families...

*A*ccentuate the positive.
*B*alance work, rest, and play.
*C*ommunicate with mutual respect.
*D*on't sweat the small stuff.
*E*ncourage healthy habits.
*F*ind ways to say "I love you."
*G*row self-esteem and
   self-acceptance.
*H*elp you do for yourself.
*I*nspire individuality and
   interdependence.
*J*uggle schedules to "be there."
*K*now there are no "perfect" families.
*L*ook for the best in each other.
*M*ake the world a better place.
*N*urture abilities and talents.

*O*penly talk about whatever's up.
*P*rovide safety and security.
*Q*uickly mend fences and move on.
*R*emind you of your uniqueness.
*S*avor memories and traditions.
*T*ake time to really listen and care.
*U*nderstand how precious "family
   time" is.
*V*alue presence more than presents.
*W*ork things out compassionately.
*X*perience life's ups and downs
   together.
*Y*earn to bequeath a spirit
   of reverence.
*Z*est to create a happy home.

©Meiji Stewart

102

Your diamonds are not in far distant mountains or in yonder seas; they are in your own backyard, if you but dig for them. *Russell H. Conwell*

Love grows by giving. The love we give away
is the only love we keep. The only way to
retain love is to give it away.

Elbert Hubbard

Animals are such agreeable friends—
they ask no questions, they pass no criticisms.

George Eliot

The thing that counts the most in the pursuit of happiness
is choosing the right traveling companion.

Friends are a second existence.

Baltasar Gracián y Morales

Friends are gifts from God. Treasure them.

You meet your friend, your face brightens—
you have struck gold. *Kassia*

It is impossible to overemphasize the immense
need human beings have to be really listened
to, to be taken seriously, to be understood.

Paul Tournier

To your good health, old friend,
may you live for a thousand years,
and I be there to count them.

Robert Smith Surtees

Grow old along with me!
The best is yet to be... *Robert Browning*

Friends are those rare people who ask how we
are and then wait to hear the answer.

Ed Cunningham

To know someone here or there with whom
you feel there is an understanding in spite of
distances or thoughts unexpressed—
that can make of this earth a garden.

Johann Wolfgang von Goethe

Do not keep the alabaster boxes of your love and tenderness
sealed up until your friends are dead. Fill their lives
with sweetness. Speak approving, cheering words while
their ears can hear them and while their hearts can be
thrilled by them. *Henry Ward Beecher*

Do not save your loving speeches
for your friends till they are dead;
do not write them on their
tombstones, speak them rather
now instead.

Anna Cummins

Of all the gifts that wise Providence grants
us to make life full and happy,
friendship is the most beautiful.

Epicurus

God's in His heaven—
All's right with the world! *Robert Browning*

The only service a friend can really render
is to keep up your courage by holding
up to you a mirror in which you can
see a noble image of yourself.

George Bernard Shaw

Wishing to be friends is quick work,
but friendship is a slow-ripening fruit.

Aristotle

A friend is one who walks in
when others walk out.

Walter Winchell

The holy passion of friendship is so
sweet and steady and loyal and enduring
in nature that it will last through a whole
lifetime, if not asked to lend money.

Mark Twain

The shoe that fits one person pinches another;
there is no recipe for living that suits all cases.

Carl Jung

If you think it's hard to meet new people,
try picking up the wrong golf ball.

Jack Lemmon

The ornaments of a house are the friends
who frequent it. *Ralph Waldo Emerson*

You never lose by loving.
You always lose by holding back.

Barbara De Angelis

Love and you shall be loved. All love is
mathematically just, as much as the two sides
of an algebraic equation.

Ralph Waldo Emerson

If the world is cold, make it your business to build fires. *Horace Traubel*

The more we give of anything,
the more we shall get back.

Grace Speare

The most precious gift that one person
can bestow upon another is
gentle encouragement.

Phillip Keller

There is nothing so rewarding as to make people realize
that they are worthwhile in this world. *Bob Anderson*

One can do without people,
but one has need of a friend.

Chinese Wisdom

My friend is one who takes me for who I am.

Henry David Thoreau

Great Spirit, grant that I may not criticize my neighbor until I have walked a mile in his moccasins. *Native American Saying*

There is no possession more valuable
than a good and faithful friend.

Socrates

No matter what looms ahead, if you can
eat today, enjoy the sunlight today,
mix good cheer with friends today,
enjoy it and bless God for it.

Henry Ward Beecher

Friendship is God's special way of loving us through someone else.

I didn't find my friends;
the good God gave them to me.

Ralph Waldo Emerson

No matter what accomplishments you achieve,
somebody helps you.

Althea Gibson

Stand outside this evening. Look at the stars.
Know that you are special and loved by
the One who created them.

Friendship is always a sweet responsibility,
never an opportunity.

Kahlil Gibran

It is great to have friends when one is young,
but indeed it is still more so when you are
getting old. When we are young, friends are,
like everything else, a matter of course. In the
old days we know what it means to have them.

Edward Grieg

We cannot tell the precise moment when
friendship formed. As in filling a vessel drop
by drop, there is at last a drop which makes it
run over; so in a series of kindnesses there is
at last one which makes the heart run over.

Samuel Johnson

Those who open their hearts to others...
are the wonderful, warmhearted people who
make the difference in our lives.

D. Manning

Soulmates...

*A*ccept you as you are.
*B*uild history together.
*C*herish being best friends.
*D*ream big dreams.
*E*nrich, comfort, and delight.
*F*all in love over and over again.
*G*row forever memories.
*H*onor feelings and needs.
*I*nvite you into their hearts.
*J*ust call to say, "I love you."
*K*now when something's up.
*L*itter love and laughter daily.
*M*ultiply joys and divide sorrows.
*N*urture your soul.

*O*vercome adversity together.
*P*ick you up when you are down.
*Q*uickly kiss and make up.
*R*emind you of your greatness.
*S*mile when they think of you.
*T*hrive on shared trust.
*U*nderstand when to "just" listen.
*V*alue independence and interdependence.
*W*alk with you when others walk away.
*X*perience ups and downs together.
*Y*earn to support your dreams.
get *Z*any together.

©Meiji Stewart

Being with you is never quite long enough.
Seeing you is never quite soon enough.
Missing you is always there. *Claudia Stewart*

Be slow in choosing a friend,
slower in changing.

Benjamin Franklin

To have a friend is to have one of the sweetest
gifts that life can bring; to be a friend is to
have a solemn and tender education of soul
from day to day.

Amy Robertson Brown

...hand
Grasps at hand, eye lights eye in good friendship, and
great hearts expand... *Robert Browning*

"Hush, don't say that—you'll lose some of
your friends." My answer is simple and final:
If I don't say it, I'll lose my own soul.

E. Stanley Jones

If...I have lost every other friend on earth,
I shall at least have one friend left, and that
friend shall be down inside of me.

Abraham Lincoln

To love a person is to learn the song that is in their heart
and to sing it to them when they have forgotten.

If you make friends with yourself, you will never be alone.

Maxwell Maltz

Some people are going to like me and some people aren't, so I might as well be me. Then, at least, I will know that the people who like, like me.

Hugh Prather

One good friend is not to be weighed against
the jewels of all the earth. *Robert South*

Love people. Use things. Not vice-versa.

Kelly Ann Rothaus

There is a universal truth that I have found
in my work. Everybody longs to be loved.
And the greatest thing we can do is let
somebody know that they are loved
and capable of loving.

Fred Rogers

Just as it is impossible to whistle and chew crackers at the same time, you cannot give love and be depressed.

A good deed is never lost;
he who sows courtesy reaps friendship,
and he who plants kindness gathers love.

Our friends see the best in us, and by that very
fact call forth the best from us.

Hugh Black

A friend is someone who comes in when the
whole world has gone out. *Emilie Barnes*

A friend may well be reckoned
the masterpiece of nature.

Ralph Waldo Emerson

What comes from the heart goes to the heart.

Samuel Taylor Coleridge

May you live all the days of your life.

Jonathan Swift

Friends...they cherish one another's hopes.
They are kind to one another's dreams.

Henry David Thoreau

The way to love anything is to realize
that it may be lost.

G. K. Chesterton

Our best friends and our worst enemies
are our thoughts. A thought can do us
more good than a doctor or a banker
or a faithful friend. It can also do us
more harm than a brick.

Frank Crane

Friendship is the only cement that will ever
hold the world together. *Woodrow Wilson*

Keep love in your heart. A life without it is like a sunless garden when the flowers are dead. The consciousness of loving and being loved brings a warmth and richness to life that nothing else can bring.

Oscar Wilde

One friend in a lifetime is much; two are many; three are hardly possible.

Henry Adams

Recipe for having friends: Be one. *Elbert Hubbard*

We are not held back by the love we didn't receive in the past, but by the love were not extending in the present.

Marianne Williamson

Take time today to call or send a grateful message to a friend.

William Arthur Ward

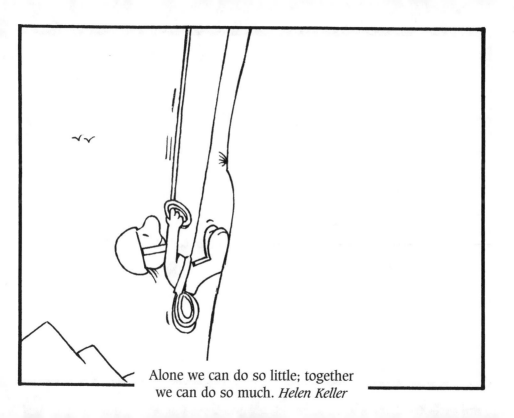

Alone we can do so little; together we can do so much. *Helen Keller*

He who has ceased to pray
has lost a great friendship.

Richard L. Evans

There is no wilderness like a life without
friends; friendship multiplies blessings and
minimizes misfortunes; it is a unique remedy
against adversity, and it soothes the soul.

Baltasar Gracián y Morales

It's co-existence or no existence. *Bertrand Russell*

In good times and bad, we need friends
who will pray for us, listen to us,
and lend a comforting hand and an
understanding ear when needed.

Beverly Lahaye

The most precious of all possessions
is a wise and loyal friend.

Darius

A friend is a present you give yourself.

Robert Louis Stevenson

Another's heart is a rare and fragile gift—
hold it gently, and with both hands.

I would be friends with you
and have your love.

William Shakespeare

It's love that makes the world go round!

W. S. Gilbert

Wherever you are it is your own friends
who make your world. *William James*

Little gift books, big messages

8313

Keep Coming Back

It gets better...
Then it gets worse...
Then it gets real...
Then it gets different...
Then it gets real different

humor & wisdom for living and loving recovery

6608

6456

6460

Little gift books, big messages

6458

6568

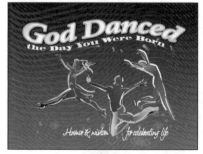

6569

6566

Little gift books, big messages

6457

6570

1737

1736

About the Author

Meiji Stewart has created other gift books, designs, and writings that may be of interest to you. Please visit www.puddledancer.com or call 1-877-EMPATHY (1-877-367-2849) for more information about any of the items listed below.

(1) **Hazelden/Keep Coming Back** - Over two hundred gift products, including greeting cards, wallet cards, bookmarks, magnets, bumper stickers, gift books, and more. (Free catalog available from Hazelden at 1-800-328-9000.)

(2) **ABC Writings** - Titles include *Children Are, Children Need, Creativity Is, Dare To, Fathers Are, Friends Are, Grandparents, Great Teachers, Happiness Is, I Am, Life Is, Loving Families, May You Always Have, Mothers Are, Recovery Is, Soulmates, Success Is,* and many more works in progress. Many of these ABC writings are available as posters (from Portal Publications) at your favorite poster and gift store, or directly from Hazelden on a variety of gift products.

(3) *Nonviolent Communication: A Language of Compassion* by Marshall Rosenberg (from PuddleDancer Press) - Jack Canfield (*Chicken Soup for the Soul* author) says, "I believe the principles and techniques in this book can literally change the world—but more importantly, they can change the quality of your life with your spouse, your children, your neighbors, your co-workers, and everyone else you interact with. I cannot recommend it highly enough." Available from Hazelden and your local and online bookstores. For more information about the Center for Nonviolent Communication call 1-800-255-7696 or visit www.cnvc.org

■ HAZELDEN®
Keep Coming Back™

Complimentary Catalog Available
Hazelden: P.O. Box 176, Center City, MN 55012-0176
1-800-328-9000   www.hazelden.org

**Hazelden/Keep Coming Back titles available from your
favorite bookstore:**

Relax, God Is in Charge	ISBN 1-56838-377-0
Keep Coming Back	ISBN 1-56838-378-9
Children Are Meant to Be Seen and Heard	ISBN 1-56838-379-7
Shoot for the Moon	ISBN 1-56838-380-0
When Life Gives You Lemons...	ISBN 1-56838-381-9
It's a Jungle Out There!	ISBN 1-56838-382-7
Parenting...Part Joy...Part Guerrilla Warfare	ISBN 1-56838-383-5
God Danced the Day You Were Born	ISBN 1-56838-384-3
Happiness Is an Inside Job	ISBN 1-56838-385-1
Anything Is Possible	ISBN 1-56838-386-X
Follow Your Dreams	ISBN 1-56838-514-5
Friends	ISBN 1-56838-515-3

Acknowledgments
Every effort has been made to find the copyright owner of the material used.
However, there are a few quotations that have been impossible to trace, and we
would be glad to hear from the copyright owners of these quotations so that
acknowledgment can be recognized in any future edition.